Can We Be Friends?
NATURE'S PARTNERS

by Alexandra Wright

illustrated by Marshall Peck III

Harcourt

Orlando   Boston   Dallas   Chicago   San Diego

Visit *The Learning Site!*
www.harcourtschool.com

To PHIL ROSANN BRUCE – MHP III

To my mother, my very best friend. – AW

This edition is published by special arrangement with Charlesbridge Publishing.

Grateful acknowledgment is made to Charlesbridge Publishing
for permission to reprint *Can We Be Friends? Nature's Partners*
by Alexandra Wright, illustrated by Marshall Peck III.
Copyright © 1994 by Charlesbridge Publishing.

Printed in the United States of America

ISBN 0-15-314368-1

1 2 3 4 5 6 7 8 9 10 060 03 02 01 00

Can We Be Friends?

This book is about some amazing animal partners.
They have learned to help each other
the way that human friends often do.
Like people who are friends, these
animals depend on each other.
They may warn one another of danger,
or help one another to hide, find food,
or stay healthy. Scientists call it symbiosis
when different animal species help
each other the way friends do.

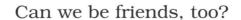

Can we be friends, too?
Before you answer, take a closer look at some of these animal partners.

DAMSEL FISH & GIANT SEA ANEMONE

A giant sea anemone looks like a flower, but it is really an animal. An anemone spends most of its life attached to a rock.

It uses its pretty tentacles to sting and eat fish that swim within reach — but not clownfish and damselfish.

This damselfish has made a layer of slime on its scales so that the anemone does not sting it.

The anemone gives the damselfish a home where it is safe. In return, the damselfish helps the anemone get food. First, the damselfish gets a bigger fish to chase it. Then, the damselfish leads the bigger fish in among the tentacles of the anemone. Time to eat!

ANTS AND APHIDS

People aren't the only ones who have farms. Ants do too, but instead of cows, they raise aphids. Aphids are little bugs that suck the juices from stems, buds, and leaves. They make a sweet liquid that ants love to drink. Ants milk their aphids just like people milk their cows.

Some ants pluck the wings off their "aphid cows" so they can't fly away. The ants herd the aphids to the best feeding spots and protect them by chasing off lady bugs, spiders, and other aphid eaters.

There are 8,000 different kinds of ants. Several million may live together in one colony. Some ants are partners with beetles, butterflies, fireflies, or birds.

CROCODILE AND EGYPTIAN PLOVER

Why isn't that crocodile eating that bird? Because the Egyptian plover is the crocodile's toothbrush and nobody, not even a twelve foot long crocodile, eats his toothbrush!

The crocodile holds his mouth open so the plover can do him the favor of cleaning all those teeth.

The plover is making a meal of the leeches, other parasites, and bits of leftover food it finds between the teeth.

Even though a crocodile eats birds, it holds very still for the plover. This crocodile also eats fish, snakes, or anything else it can catch. His big sister eats antelope, zebra, warthogs, and, sometimes, even people.

RATEL AND HONEY GUIDE

What a lot of noise this honey guide bird is making! It is trying to get the attention of a badger-like animal, called a ratel. The ratel finally notices what is making that high-pitched churring call. It follows the bird through the bushes and over the rocks because it knows that the bird is leading it to a beehive.

The ratel tears
the hive
apart with its
sharp claws and
laps up the honey.
Thick, rubbery skin
protects it from bee
stings. The bird waits its turn
to eat the leftover honeycomb.
Beeswax is its favorite food. Yum, yum!

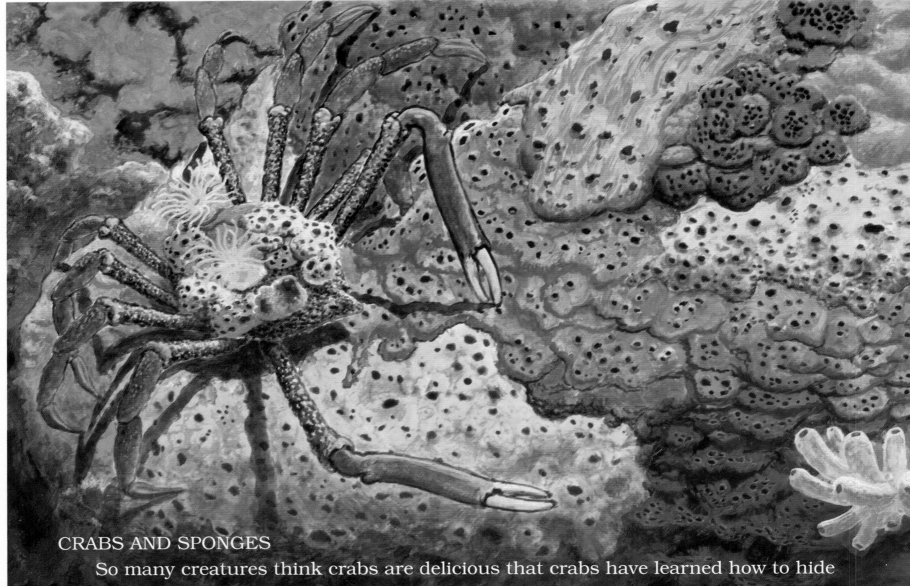

CRABS AND SPONGES

So many creatures think crabs are delicious that crabs have learned how to hide even when they are out in the open. Decorator crabs hide by covering their shells with sponges and other small animals that usually grow on rocks.

As the crab walks around, the sponges and other animals have an easy time getting food, and the crab escapes its enemies by looking like just another rock.

This decorator crab has moved into an area where a lot of anemones live and green seaweed grows, so it is adding some of each to its costume. If it leaves this area, it will probably take them off again and find some new camouflage.

OSTRICH AND ZEBRA

Slowly, the lioness moves closer and closer. Carefully she creeps toward her next meal. The zebras have picked up her scent. They flare their nostrils and paw the ground. It is a signal for the zebras and ostriches to begin to move away . . . slowly at first. Then all at once, they break into a 30-mile-an-hour gallop.

Another day the ostriches will warn the zebras. An eight-foot-tall ostrich can see a lion more easily than a five-foot-tall zebra can. The ostrich has bigger eyes than any other bird or land animal! To keep out dust and dirt, it has an eyelid that closes sideways which it can see right through!

SYMBIOTIC FISH

Even fish have to go to the doctor! This yellow-tailed goatfish is sick. Its red spots show the "doctor" where it hurts. The doctor, a young French angel fish, gets a good meal by eating the fungus, bacteria, or parasites that it finds on its "patients." Several hundred fish may be seen by a "doctor" in one day.

Wrasses, gobis, and other kinds of fish are "doctors," too. Generally, the "doctors" have stripes and bright colors, and some do a little dance so that their "patients" can find them underwater.

Some "patients" will roll over on their sides or stand on their heads to show that they are not going to eat the "doctor."

SOOTY SHEARWATER AND TUATARA

Taking turns is what the sooty shearwater and the tuatara do best.
When the shearwater flies away in the morning, the tuatara crawls
into the shearwater's tunnel to sleep. The tuatara keeps the
tunnel clean by eating any beetles, flies, or spiders
that come in.

When the shearwater comes
home at night to sleep,
the tuatara goes
out to hunt.

In winter, the shearwater migrates and the tuatara hibernates in the nest. This home sharing may have helped the tuatara survive long enough to become a living fossil. Its only relatives are the dinosaurs that lived 150 million years ago. It has a third eye on the top of its head and is the only reptile with a beak!

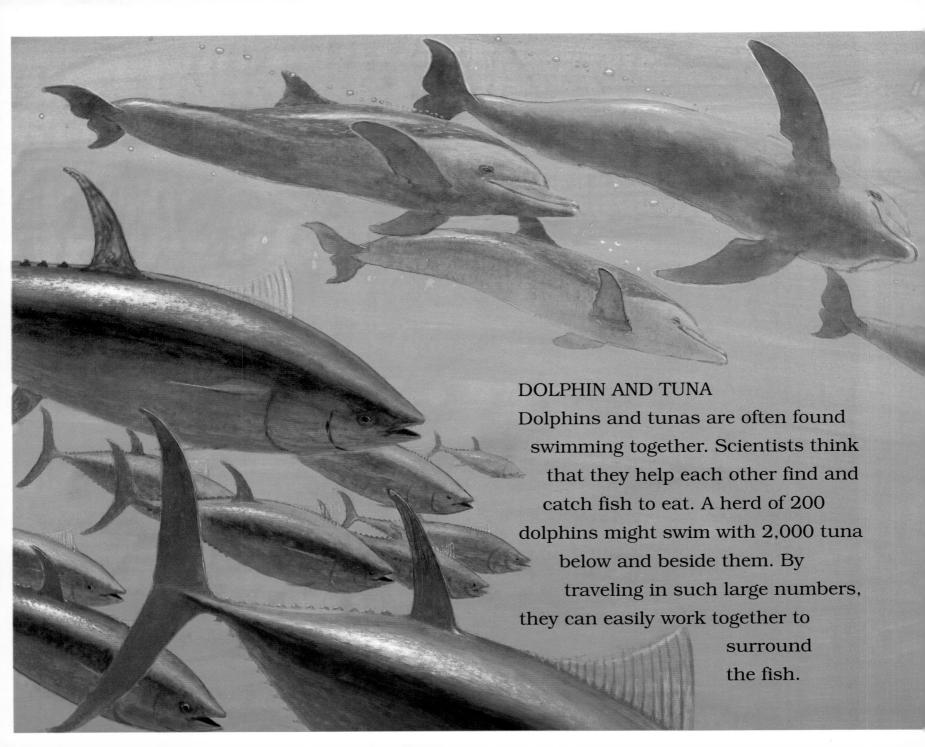

DOLPHIN AND TUNA

Dolphins and tunas are often found swimming together. Scientists think that they help each other find and catch fish to eat. A herd of 200 dolphins might swim with 2,000 tuna below and beside them. By traveling in such large numbers, they can easily work together to surround the fish.

Dolphins are mammals. They hunt by making sounds that are about 100 times higher than the sounds that fish can hear. The sounds bounce off the fish and come back to the dolphins, so the dolphins know where the fish are. These dolphins have just found some tasty flying fish. The flying fish try to escape by leaping right out of the water, but they can only "fly" for about 100 feet before plunging back into the waves.

Fishing boats used to set nets around these dolphins to catch the tuna.

The dolphins were often killed as a result, but so many people protested that different methods are now used. Cans of tuna often say "dolphin-safe" on the label.

AFRICAN RHINO AND RED-BILLED OXPECKER

What is that little bird doing sitting on that rhino's head? The bird eats the pesky bugs that bite the rhino. Each bird takes care of its own particular rhino. Even though the bird will leave to mate and raise a family, it will come back to its own special friend.

The red-billed oxpecker has special hooked toes so that it can climb all over its friend without falling off. This ability to hang upside-down helps it find a meal of bugs even when the rhino is moving.

Rhinos have no enemies other than people who want only the rhino horn. A rhino's horn can grow to over five feet long and is made of the same material as our fingernails (keratin). Imagine having a 5 foot fingernail growing out of your nose!

RUFOUS WOODPECKER AND BLACK TREE ANT

If you go to India, do not touch any black tree ants because they bite. These ants make a nest that hangs from a tree. Most birds won't nest in that tree because these ants eat bird eggs.

The ants' worst enemy is the rufous woodpecker, which eats hundreds of ants at every meal.

During nesting time, the bird makes peace with the ants, and they share the same tree. The woodpecker digs a hole in the trunk of the tree and lays its eggs. It does not eat the ants and the ants don't bother its eggs. Every year they demonstrate how even enemies can become peaceful when they need to be.

GIRAFFE AND WILDEBEEST

When you are the tallest of all living animals, it is hard to get a drink. A giraffe's long neck and 18-inch-long tongue are not quite long enough to reach the water. It has to stand with its front legs at a wide angle. It can go for an entire month without a drink, but when it gets thirsty, it drinks about ten gallons at a time! A drinking giraffe cannot see whether there are any dangerous animals sneaking up!

Fortunately, giraffes have friends. The wildebeests and even
some impalas keep watch while the giraffe drinks.
The giraffe repays the favor by being the lookout
while the others drink or graze.

Even if an enemy does sneak up close,
it will probably be confused by the
thundering mass of different sizes,
shapes, scents, and hoofbeats.

KORI BUSTARD AND CARMINE BEE EATER

Hello, big bird! The kori bustard is the heaviest of the flying birds. It weighs as much as 40 pounds and is over three feet tall. It has a good friend, the carmine bee eater. When the kori bustard goes out for a walk, it takes its friend along for the ride.

The carmine bee eater sits in comfort. During their walk, the carmine bee eater may eat a few of the insects that annoy its partner. As the bustard walks around looking for mice and grasshoppers to eat, it seems to enjoy the company of the little bird. Perhaps, like people, these birds have come to appreciate companionship, the way some people enjoy the company of their pets.

Can we be friends?
Now that you have seen the ways
that animals have learned
to be friends, don't you think
that we can, too?

To be their friends, we need to learn how to
share the Earth with the animals – to
save the forests, beaches, fields, and
streams where the animals live, and to
make less pollution.

Even though animal partners may be different
in looks, color, size, and shape, they work together
in harmony. We can learn a great deal from these
animal friends.

Like the giant sea anemone, we can protect friends
who are smaller. Like the sooty shearwater and tuatara,
we can share our possessions, take turns, and work out
solutions so that everyone is comfortable. Like the
ostrich and the zebra, we can look out for each
other and use our special abilities to help each other.
Like the kori bustard and the carmine bee eater, we can
enjoy each other's companionship.

We can
learn from
these animals how
to live together even though
we may have different needs,
goals, or appearances.
The one goal that we can all
share is to live in harmony
with every other living thing.
So, don't step on that ant or chase that bird.
Watch it and study how it lives.
Who knows? It may become your partner in nature.